THIS NOTEBOOK BELONGS TO:

Made in the USA
Las Vegas, NV
11 January 2021

15736963R00083